Through Dark Rivers

A Journey through Loss to Joy

by Susan Erikson

Copyright © 2011, 2012 revised, by Susan Erikson
All rights reserved.

Unless otherwise indicated all Scripture quotations are from The Holy Bible, English Standard Version ® (ESV®), copyright © 2001 by Crossway Bibles, a publishing ministry of Good News Publishers. Used by permission. All rights reserved.

The "ESV" and "English Standard Version" are registered trademarks of Good News Publishers. Use of either trademark requires the permission of Good New Publishers.

Scripture taken from the HOLY BIBLE, NEW INTERNATIONAL VERSION ®. Copyright © 1973, 1978, 1984 by International Bible Society. Used by permission of Zondervan Publishing House. All rights reserved.

The "NIV" and "New International Version" trademarks are registered in the United States Patent and Trademark Office by International Bible Society. Use of either trademark requires the permission of International Bible Society.

All hymns are in public domain

No portion of this book may be reproduced in any way without the written permission of the author, except for brief excerpts in magazine reviews, etc.

ISBN 978-0-615-42081-3

Photo Art

by Marilyn Segaves

Isaiah 40: 28-31

Have you not known? Have you not heard? The LORD is the everlasting God, the Creator of the ends of the earth. He does not faint or grow weary; his understanding is unsearchable. He gives power to the faint, and to him who has no might he increases strength. Even youths shall faint and be weary, and young men shall fall exhausted; but they who wait for the LORD shall renew their strength; they shall mount up with wings like eagles; they shall run and not be weary; they shall walk and not faint.

TABLE OF CONTENTS

LOSS OVERWHELMS 10

THE BIRTH OF LOSS AND THE
BEGINNINGS OF RESCUE 14

TRUSTING CHRIST IN LOSS 30

FINDING HOPE THROUGH LOSS 50

LIVING BY GRACE THROUGH LOSS 70

THE DEATH OF LOSS
AND THE BIRTH OF JOY 100

Psalm 23*

The covenant LORD, Christ, is my King,
And I shall never have needs He cannot meet.
He makes me lie down in contented and sure rest;
He leads me to where the water is good, and refreshing,
where He restores my soul.
He guides me in the right paths,
conforming me to His good will.
Even though I may find myself shadowed by death and loss,
I will not be afraid, for I am not alone.
He is always with me.
His protection is secure and comforting.
I know I am under His protection,
because He has invited me to sit at His table.
He has offered me all the benefits of an honored guest,
And these benefits are extravagantly generous.
Surely God will chase me down
all the days of my life,
Offering me His goodness, His love, and His
   covenant faithfulness.
And because of Christ, I will dwell in His house for all eternity.

---

*Author's paraphrase

Isaiah 50:10

Who among you fears the LORD and obeys the voice of his servant? Let him who walks in darkness and has no light trust in the name of the LORD and rely on his God.

Isaiah 51:1-3

Listen to me, you who pursue righteousness, you who seek the LORD: look to the rock from which you were hewn, and to the quarry from which you were dug. Look to Abraham your father and to Sarah who bore you; for he was but one when I called him, that I might bless him and multiply him. For the LORD comforts Zion; he comforts all her waste places and makes her wilderness like Eden, her desert like the garden of the LORD; joy and gladness will be found in her, thanksgiving and the voice of song.

10

LOSS OVERWHELMS

"Need Help to Get Home"

He's probably homeless,
Squatting by the Arby's
Where every driver going by can see his sign:

"Need help to get home."

And I'm thinking,
Avoid eye contact.
What good is a friendly smile when I
Can't give him a ride?

And then I see myself in God's eyes,
Squatting by the cosmic road,
Seen in all the righteous spots
So every Christian going by can see it's Me.

And I realize, I too am holding up a ragged sign:

"Need help to get home."

Only
God is the only one who really sees.

I've draped my sign with platitudes
and hymnal shine,
With sequined Scripture, words and deeds.
Theology of Sunday's best,
With family pride and sparkling wit.
You'd think no one would see the rest.

But there's my sign,
Like neon flashing in God's face:

"Need help to get home."

I Have a Name

I'm not a box
of sifting names.

I have collected categories,
Title-Works
throughout the years –
Mommy,
Honey,
Daughter,
Scholar,
Music-maker,
Wife and lover,
"You're-the-one-who-spoke-at-church,"
"I've-seen-you-with-the Children's-Choir."

"It's what you do,"
The people say,
And I have done a lot of things.

But what if
place and people change?
And children grow and move away?
Or loved ones die?
Or bodies suffer time's decay,
and all the little details naming life
become undone
and undesired,
a trembling consequence of age,
of plans unfinished,
parts and pieces carried to another page,
all titles dashed,
Where once was work
and what was name
now lie in ash?

What then?
of drifting names –
This one today,
That one remaining
once the rest have blown away.

I'm not a box.
I have a name.

THE BIRTH OF LOSS AND THE BEGINNINGS OF RESCUE

What arrogance is there in one who daily dialogues with God without humility, without the sense of the Gospel's weight, the weight of blood? Do we realize it is a cosmically momentous grace to the undeserving?

The Gift

His swollen face,
Almost a face one cannot read
or comprehend,
Is caught between old shoulders
Crushed,
Wide-stretched.
His arms encompass all the dark
of fear and dread,
An ugliness that
Screams for blood and crowns his head.

And He hangs
Cramped,
Against the tree,
As shadows slip,
They slip away,
He slips away,

All this for me.

RESCUE

Stricken, Smitten, and Afflicted
Thomas Kelly, 1804

Stricken, smitten, and afflicted, see him dying on the tree!
'Tis the Christ by man rejected; yes, my soul, 'tis he, 'tis he!
'Tis the long expected Prophet, David's son, yet David's Lord;
By his Son God now has spoken: 'tis the true and faithful Word.

Tell me, ye who hear him groaning, was there ever grief like his?
Friends thro' fear his cause disowning, foes insulting his distress;
Many hands were raised to wound him, none would interpose to save;
But the deepest stroke that pierced him was the stroke that Justice gave.

Ye who think of sin but lightly nor suppose the evil great
Here may view its nature rightly, here its guilt may estimate.
Mark the sacrifice appointed, see who bears the awful load;
'tis the Word, the Lord's anointed, son of Man and Son of God.

Armageddon

Who could stand
the thundering Wind that blew from Har Magedon
down the path toward sin,
toward Adam's sin?
Relentless Breath that sobbed betrayal,
Judgment's tears all raining death
on covered heads already cursed.

And yet

The worst was turned aside.
The wayward son,
Restrained,
Renamed
until the Wind himself could ride a fiery chariot into War,
A Holy War,
Where even death would smell the dragon's stench of shame,
and He Who Is would swallow wrath that had been meant
for Adam's kin,
would peel away the coffin skin that sheltered pain.

RESCUE

Day of Reckoning

Eve

A winter dragon
whispered in great-grandma's ear.
Its icy lips raised fantasies of kingdom
   glories,
Mighty Works
(all endless gray phantasms only egos hear).
And she who bit
was bitten more,
Forgetting sighs and dragon tears
are empty smoke,
Enticing lies meant to provoke
the careless heart.
And she who prostituted self
for dragon's wealth,
embraced instead on pain of death,
An empty lie, a bitter laugh.

Adam

He thought he was Apollo,
Flaming prince of endless might.
But he mistook a mourning star
for Heaven's light,
Exchanging lies for cosmic dreams,
Burning lies whose great inferno
swallowed him in smoldering ash,
A thousand altars of regret,
An endless ziggurat of blame
That cried out darkness,
cold,
and shame.
No fires left, no blazing throne.
All vanity,
The man
Alone
(like flickering shadows
dancing on the edge of light),
An echo of forgottenness,
forgotten dreams,
forgotten Name,

Where only empty cold remains.

Fear the cold
That seeps within the selfish soul,
That swallows heart in icy pride,
And does not dread the winter white
that hides the deed,
Entombing light.

RESCUE

And There Was Evening
and There Was Mourning

It used to be that dark
was only opposite to light.
But that was life
Before the Fall,
Before rebellion
sliced the dark in gruesome shapes
to build a wall.

And blocks of fear and guilty shame
were mortared in by human blood,
Foundations laid,
Embedded dark in fratricide,
Where boasts of murder,
Like graffiti,
Marred the gates,
And barred the Gardeners
From their claims on innocence,
Their right to fellowship with light.

Now penalties and crimes
Inscribed corrupting pride,
And death instead
Became the opposite of day.

And Man and Woman found two roads –
Imbibe the dark,
Where Justice metes eternal pains,
Or
Rest in Blood, in Holy Blood.
Let Sacrifice against
the flood of sorrows laid in rows of stone,
Become the Executioner's stay.

O Sacred Head, Now Wounded
Bernard of Clairvaux, 1091-1153

O sacred Head, now wounded, with grief and shame
   weighed down;
Now scornfully surrounded with thorns, thine only
   crown;
O sacred head, what glory, what bliss till now was thine!
Yet, though despised and gory, I joy to call thee mine.

What thou, my Lord, hast suffered was all for sinners'
   gain:
Mine, mine was the transgression, but thine the deadly
   pain.
Lo, here I fall, my Savior! 'Tis I deserve thy place;
Look on me with thy favor, vouchsafe to me thy grace.

Song of the Heart

Eve, Eve,
come off the grave.
You cannot whisper Abel back,
Your weeping cannot raise his head,
Or breathing incantations
make new soul from dirt.
Your sighs name blood already spent,
whose bleeding seeps through aching earth.
Too soon, too soon
has woman's heart enveloped hurt.
One son to dust,
One son in covenant with death.
Too soon, too soon
the woman's curse has touched the son.
Too soon the man regrets the deed already done.
Familial love is now decayed,
Until the day when
He Who Slays defends the dead from dragon's worst,
And He delivers life from pain,
A new creation,
   Someday mixing Abel's dust with blood and breath.
.

RESCUE

Jesus, Lover of My Soul
Charles Wesley, 1740

Jesus, lover of my soul, let me to thy bosom fly,
While the nearer waters roll, while the tempest still is high:
Hide me, O my Savior, hide, till the storm of life is past;
Safe into the haven guide, O receive my soul at last!

Other refuge have I none, hangs my helpless soul on thee;
Leave, ah! Leave me not alone, still support and comfort me!
All my trust on thee is stayed, all my help from thee I bring;
Cover my defenseless head with the shadow of thy wing.

Plenteous grace with thee is found, grace to cover all my sin;
Let the healing streams abound; make and keep me pure within:
Thou of life the fountain art, freely let me take of thee;
Spring thou up within my heart, rise to all eternity.

Romans 8:1-11

There is therefore now no condemnation for those who are in Christ Jesus. For the law of the Spirit of life has set you free in Christ Jesus from the law of sin and death. For God has done what the law, weakened by the flesh, could not do. By sending his own Son in the likeness of sinful flesh and for sin, he condemned sin in the flesh, in order that the righteous requirement of the law might be fulfilled in us, who walk not according to the flesh but according to the Spirit. For those who live according to the flesh set their minds on the things of the flesh, but those who live according to the Spirit set their minds on the things of the Spirit. For to set the mind on the flesh is death, but to set the mind on the Spirit is life and peace. For the mind that is set on the flesh is hostile to God, for it does not submit to God's law; indeed, it cannot. Those who are in the flesh cannot please God. You, however, are not in the flesh but in the Spirit, if in fact the Spirit of God dwells in you. Anyone who does not have the Spirit of Christ does not belong to him. But if Christ is in you, although the body is dead because of sin, the Spirit is life because of righteousness. If the Spirit of him who raised Jesus from the dead dwells in you, he who raised Christ Jesus from the dead will also give life to your mortal bodies through his Spirit who dwells in you.

Seasons

Eden's Summer breathes in peace across my face.
A hint of sun,
A whiff of grace,
'til shivering thoughts (like lost primordial memories)
fill the space.

Lamenting sorrows
"Blood for blood!"

And I remember why I cannot capture sun,
or sift rich dirt through eager hands,
but only peer (half in a dream)
through garden walls at brilliant stalks.
Toward what I knew and cannot hold,
To what I need and cannot own,
but stand bereft,
A prince of cold,
A princess heaping endless stones to pleasured death,
with flaming heaven guarding guilt.

Eden's Autumn tastes of ash,
Cremated glories linger past
a hint of leaves,
a whiff of smoke.
The browning edge on creeping weeds,
The tired sway of bending grass
too long,
too old,
too soon invoking sighs of dusk,
Exhaling earth releasing dark.
Relentless bleeding soaks and rends.
If only lambs could bring an end,
If only rams could staunch the flow,
If only man could scale the wall
and bring the garden back before
the raging waters fell and cried,
before the ancient meadows died,
before the Guilt.

Eden's Winter sharpens pain,
where even churching cannot warm
or cover up the spreading stain.

He stands,
The Heart of Heaven's Love,
Between my guilt and Eden's wall.
He is the blood to answer blood.
What lambs cannot,
This Lamb has done.
My spirit groans and yearns to hold what lies beyond
the garden's gate.
And He who warms the coldest heart,
Who walks in time 'til age unraveling comes to end,
Will someday speak and shatter stone,
Inviting tendered hearts to mend.

'Til Eden's Spring
brings lasting peace,
and gardening waits,
He brings the rain
to flower fields,
to quench the thirst of arid earth.
He lends the wind to favor grass.
He blows His Breath across my face,
The warmth of sun,
A wealth of grace.

RESCUE

Flowers of the Field

Psalm 103:15-16 As for man, his days are like grass; he flourishes like a flower of the field; the wind passes over it, and it is gone, and its place knows it no more.

This world gathers peoples up
in vast bouquets,
A field of bright and florid flowers
bunched and grouped
By race,
By pain,
By hubris feeding cold disdain,
By fears of grand oppression
making ragged crowds of alienation,
Each man standing all alone,
Yet hoping standing one to one
will overcome the walls,
The wars that crumble hearts.

And throwing darts on other blooms
becomes a solidarity of might
where WE are right,
Our righteous power conquering wrongs.

And yet each flower
blows away on nature's wind,
Each bright bouquet
eventually folds crumbling into
Wasted silence,
Earth's decay,
Discarded memories and song,
With each man standing
Still alone,
His voice is gone,
His hopes forgotten by a world
that gathers hearts and buries dreams
of fellowship in crypts and stone.
Into this energy of lives,

Relentlessly pursuing ties that lead to dust,
Comes One who truly knows
Our finite selves,
Our disconnected, broken hearts.
He knows our striving,
Wasting, scrambling rush
to race against an empty death.

He knows.

And into faces shouting prideful breath,
He breathes His peace,
His blood,
His sacrifice,
Himself the reconciliation man has sought,
Illusively beyond all grasps
but His.

This One,
The Christ,
He is the Gatherer
folding fragile blooms in love
before the Cross,
with hands engraved by human scars
of sin and pain,
His own heart pierced
for our disdain.
And blood and water melting
stones of alienation,
Men and women finally burst forgotten tombs.
And in this New Creation
Flourish,
Growing into grace together,
Vast bouquets
Forever coloring into
glorious shades,
The hills and fields of God's domain.

RESCUE

TRUSTING CHRIST IN LOSS

Parenting in God's universe, it seems, is about trust under fire.

Isaiah 43:1-7

But now thus says the L ORD, he who created you, O Jacob, he who formed you, O Israel: "Fear not, for I have redeemed you; I have called you by name, you are mine. When you pass through the waters, I will be with you; and through the rivers, they shall not overwhelm you; when you walk through fire you shall not be burned, and the flame shall not consume you. For I am the L ORD your God, the Holy One of Israel, your Savior. I give Egypt as your ransom, Cush and Seba in exchange for you. Because you are precious in my eyes, and honored, and I love you, I give men in return for you, peoples in exchange for your life. Fear not, for I am with you; I will bring your offspring from the east, and from the west I will gather you. I will say to the north, Give up, and to the south, Do not withhold; bring my sons from afar and my daughters from the end of the earth, everyone who is called by my name, whom I created for my glory, whom I formed and made."

TRUST

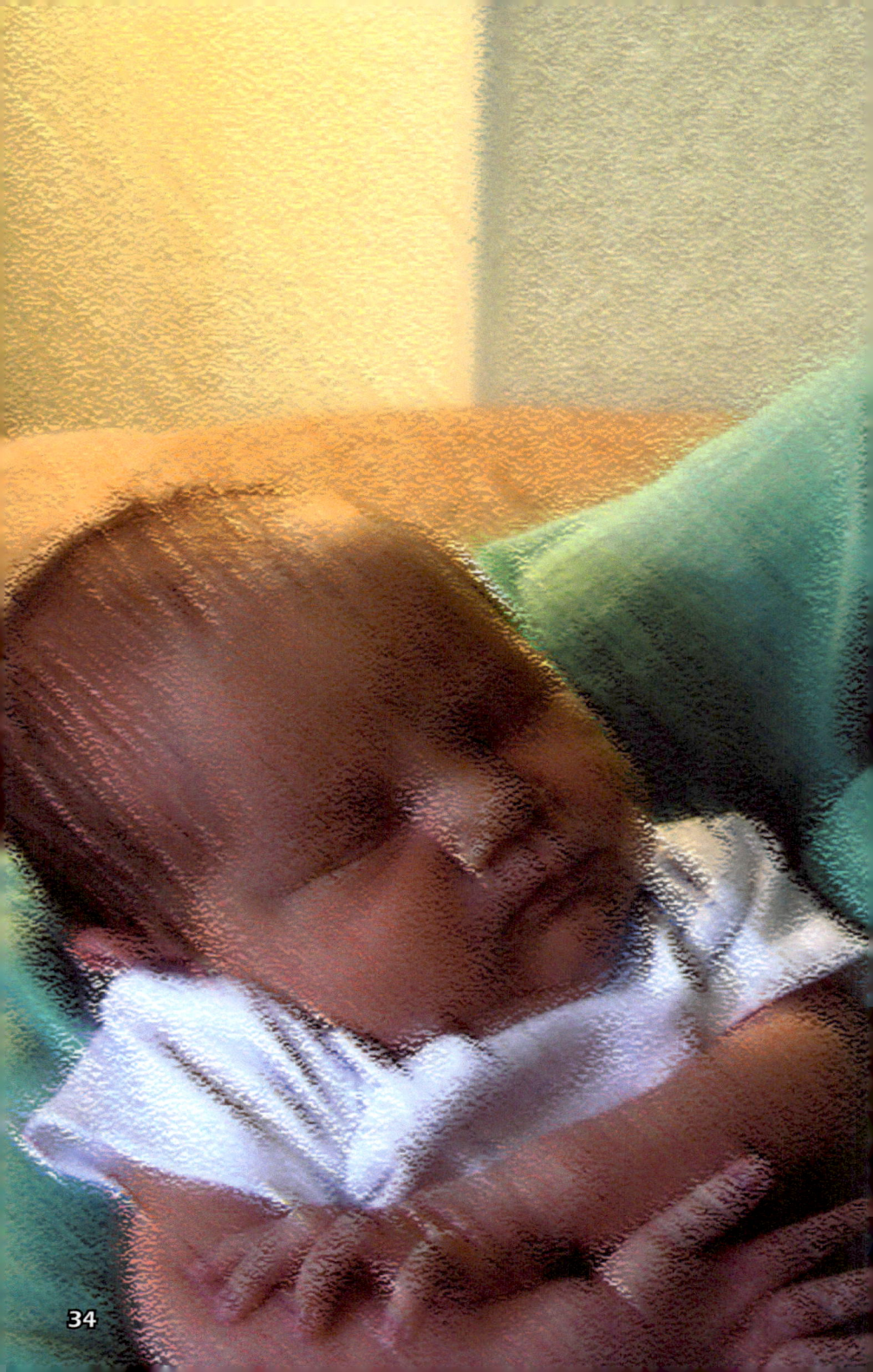

God's Holy Arm

His tiny heart
beats close to me,
All wrapped in baby,
Back to nose,
With button toes,
Still blue,
Still new,
Still just begun at being boy.

He has not known the agony,
He has not even sensed my joy.

For one last time
we rock as one,
And then I start to give him back
And find
We both are cradled still,
In God's own hands,
In God's own will.

TRUST

Second Thoughts

He gave her to me
Babe to breast,
And then he reached his waiting hand
to take her back.

And I, like Rachel,
Fell and cried,
and would not let her go.

But she was only mine
to have and hold
'til death could part her hand from mine,
And put her tiny hand in his,
And how could I name Becky's time?

Baby's Breath

Pardon me,
I thought my son belonged to me,
To care
To raise until the age when he could stand without my love,
Without my heart and help.

But here I stand,
Apart,
Alone,
His feet don't even touch the floor,
Already barren,
And he already spoken for.

TRUST

Waiting

"Wait on Him," He says to us,
And so we wait.
We carry waiting's weighted rooms,
all burdens borne by wearied hearts,
And balance faith with parents' fears,
Where waiting sharpens doubts and glooms.

Will CAT scans bruise a child's delight?
Or cancer's threading
bind our tears to wretching night?

This little child is one of us,
Our bigger hands in smaller size,
Our loopy grins,
Our grinning eyes
now waiting, hopeful
we can hold her sorrows back
with human arms,
with prayers and sighs.

And so we find ourselves
Outside ourselves
at Heaven's door.

For human arms are good for love,
For joyful hugs
and holding tight.
But human arms can never conquer
Cancer's war,
Nor lock the gate
from all that threatens this child's life.

And so we wait.

"Wait on Him," He says again.
And father-mother
walk with daughter
down the path the Lord has set,
And trust His arms to carry ours
Toward paths unknown
Toward patient trust,
Toward promises and wakings' end.

O Love That Wilt Not Let Me Go
George Matheson, 1882

O Love that wilt not let me go, I rest my weary soul in thee;
I give thee back the life I owe, that in thine ocean depths its flow may richer, fuller be.

O Light that follow'st all my way, I yield my flick'ring torch to thee;
My heart restores its borrowed ray, that in thy sunshine's blaze its day may brighter, fairer be.

O Joy that seekest me through pain, I cannot close my heart to thee;
I trace the rainbow through the rain, and feel the promise is not vain that morn shall tearless be.

O Cross that liftest up my head, I dare not ask to fly from thee;
I lay in dust life's glory dead, and from the ground there blossoms red life that shall endless be.

Psalm 13

How long, O Lord? Will you forget me forever? How long will you hide your face from me? How long must I take counsel in my soul and have sorrow in my heart all the day? How long shall my enemy be exalted over me?

Consider and answer me, O Lord my God; light up my eyes, lest I sleep the sleep of death, lest my enemy say, "I have prevailed over him," lest my foes rejoice because I am shaken.

But I have trusted in your steadfast love; my heart shall rejoice in your salvation. I will sing to the Lord, because he has dealt bountifully with me.

Psalm 18:1-2

I love you, O Lord, my strength. The Lord is my rock and my fortress and my deliverer, my God, my rock, in whom I take refuge, my shield, and the horn of my salvation, my stronghold.

TRUST

So Goes the Dance

Come baby-waltz at two a.m.,
The mother, child, dance chest to chest,
Two hearts caressed in whispered dreams,
The one beguiled
By mewing child,
By love unseen –
So Goes the Dance.

And then comes school,
Where dreaming grows
in ballet pink and purple bows,
Where dolls and dresses shape the face
in innocence and childish grace.
And mother, child, walk hand in hand,
Amending steps –
So Goes the Dance.

Two steps forward, five steps back.
Bleeding adolescence wounds
a restless heart.
The child is woman,
Woman,
Child,
The dance dissolves in tender traps
'til one is left.
The mother lingering, arms bereft –
So Goes the Dance.

But still she waits, a partner yet.
A mother knows
She cannot hold or replay steps already spent.
But someday dreams may need a friend,
A woman's heart,
A woman's hand,
A gentle waltz to steady steps.
Until that day she'll take her stance –
So Goes the Dance.

TRUST

So These are the Leaner Years

What if he goes?
(This child of me,
my progeny).
What if he walks away from Faith?
Away from all the tender songs
and words I heard when he was four,
When life was "Jesus loves me"
whispered by the door,
And grand theology was flung
in sing-song voice
from earth to sky on playground swings,
And I thought parenting was all about
Good church,
Good schools,
Where I could mold elusive wings
on children made of my own clay.

Oh, we are fools
who dote and praise on babies' hearts,
Forgetting each comes
full-blown sinner into life,
And we ourselves,
All bent from birth,
Are not exempt from all the flaws
that mix our messages of faith,
And scramble sacredness with strife.

This child,
Whose adolescence plays our worried souls,
Whose early whispers
now come shouting out disdain,
Cannot out-shout our Lord and King,
Nor overpower
He Who Molded Everything,
He hold's our offspring's molecules
in perfect place,
He breathes Himself
into this rebel
straining at the edge of Grace.

What if he goes?
This time I think,
"Then let him go."
And pray for Providence
To chase this prodigal toward Christ,
Toward faithful promises once
proven out by sacrifice,
By "He Who Saves,"
Who fathers fearful, bending hearts,
And mends both child
And parent parts
In ancient Covenant's embrace.

TRUST

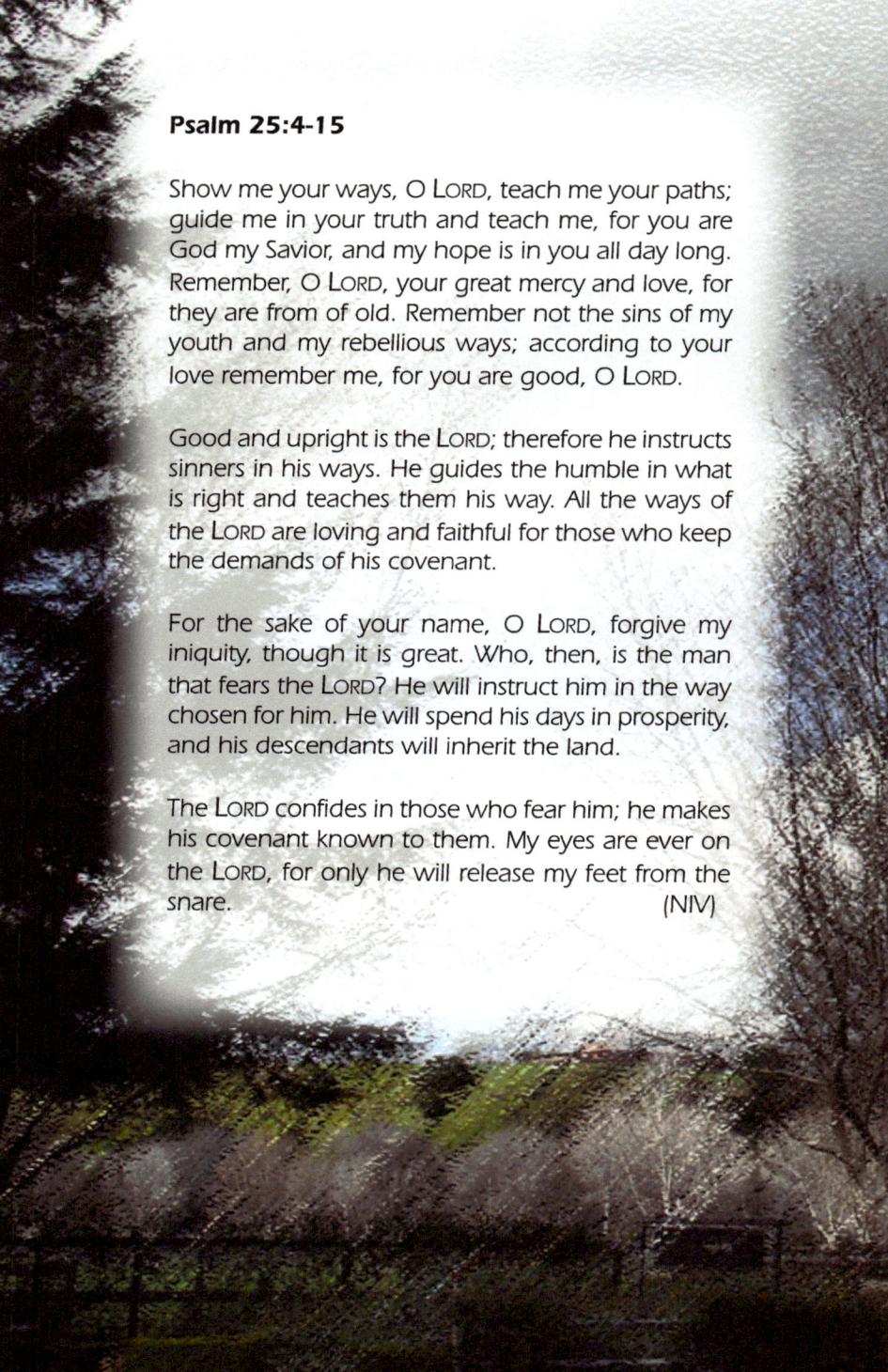

Psalm 25:4-15

Show me your ways, O LORD, teach me your paths; guide me in your truth and teach me, for you are God my Savior, and my hope is in you all day long. Remember, O LORD, your great mercy and love, for they are from of old. Remember not the sins of my youth and my rebellious ways; according to your love remember me, for you are good, O LORD.

Good and upright is the LORD; therefore he instructs sinners in his ways. He guides the humble in what is right and teaches them his way. All the ways of the LORD are loving and faithful for those who keep the demands of his covenant.

For the sake of your name, O LORD, forgive my iniquity, though it is great. Who, then, is the man that fears the LORD? He will instruct him in the way chosen for him. He will spend his days in prosperity, and his descendants will inherit the land.

The LORD confides in those who fear him; he makes his covenant known to them. My eyes are ever on the LORD, for only he will release my feet from the snare. (NIV)

Whate'er My God Ordains Is Right
Samuel Rodigast, 1675

Whate'er my God ordains is right: his holy will abideth;
I will be still whate'er he doth, and follow where he guideth.
He is my God; though dark my road, he holds me that I shall not fall:
Wherefore to him I leave it all.

Whate'er my God ordains is right: he never will deceive me;
He leads me by the proper path; I know he will not leave me.
I take, content, what he hath sent; his hand can turn my griefs away,
And patiently I wait his day.

Whate'er my God ordains is right: here shall my stand be taken;
Though sorrow, need, or death be mine, yet am I not forsaken.
My Father's care is round me there; he holds me that I shall not fall:
And so to him I leave it all.

TRUST

My Empty House

My empty house
makes solitude a boisterous noise,
A cacophony of memory in glorious bloom.
I can't forget,
I can't deny this quiet cry
some days, some hours,
for other times,
For places done and gone too fast,
Where echoed memories
waver past,
For younger thoughts not quite forgotten,
(older now without a child to smile a room.)

My meager list
(ironic twist that I should find myself too weary now,
or needing rest,)
Instead of story time and runny noses,
One more hug
before my light and energy gives way,
(too slow without a child to hurry up my endless day.)

I am Between,
A mother still toward infant thoughts
and wonderment in simple things,
Grandmother more for solitude,
For memories and empty swings.
I'll hold a little hand again,
A little while,
And breathe the air of energy and reckless hearts,
Then back to silence,
Sad as disconnecting noisy moments cease,
Yet eagerly and childless now,
Embracing peace.

ism # FINDING HOPE THROUGH LOSS

I hate the word, "cancer."
It takes the air out of the room.

HOPE

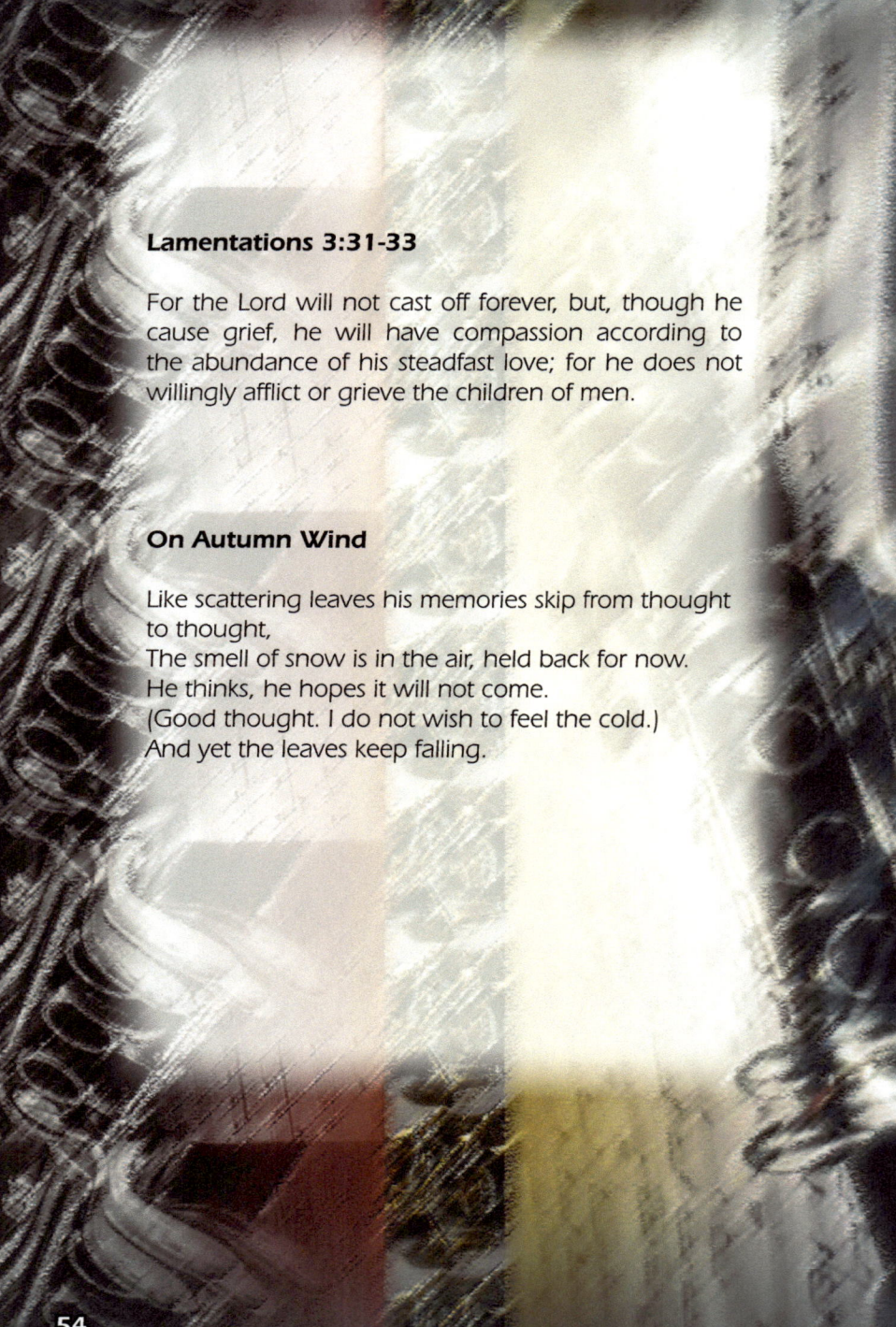

Lamentations 3:31-33

For the Lord will not cast off forever, but, though he cause grief, he will have compassion according to the abundance of his steadfast love; for he does not willingly afflict or grieve the children of men.

On Autumn Wind

Like scattering leaves his memories skip from thought to thought,
The smell of snow is in the air, held back for now.
He thinks, he hopes it will not come.
(Good thought. I do not wish to feel the cold.)
And yet the leaves keep falling.

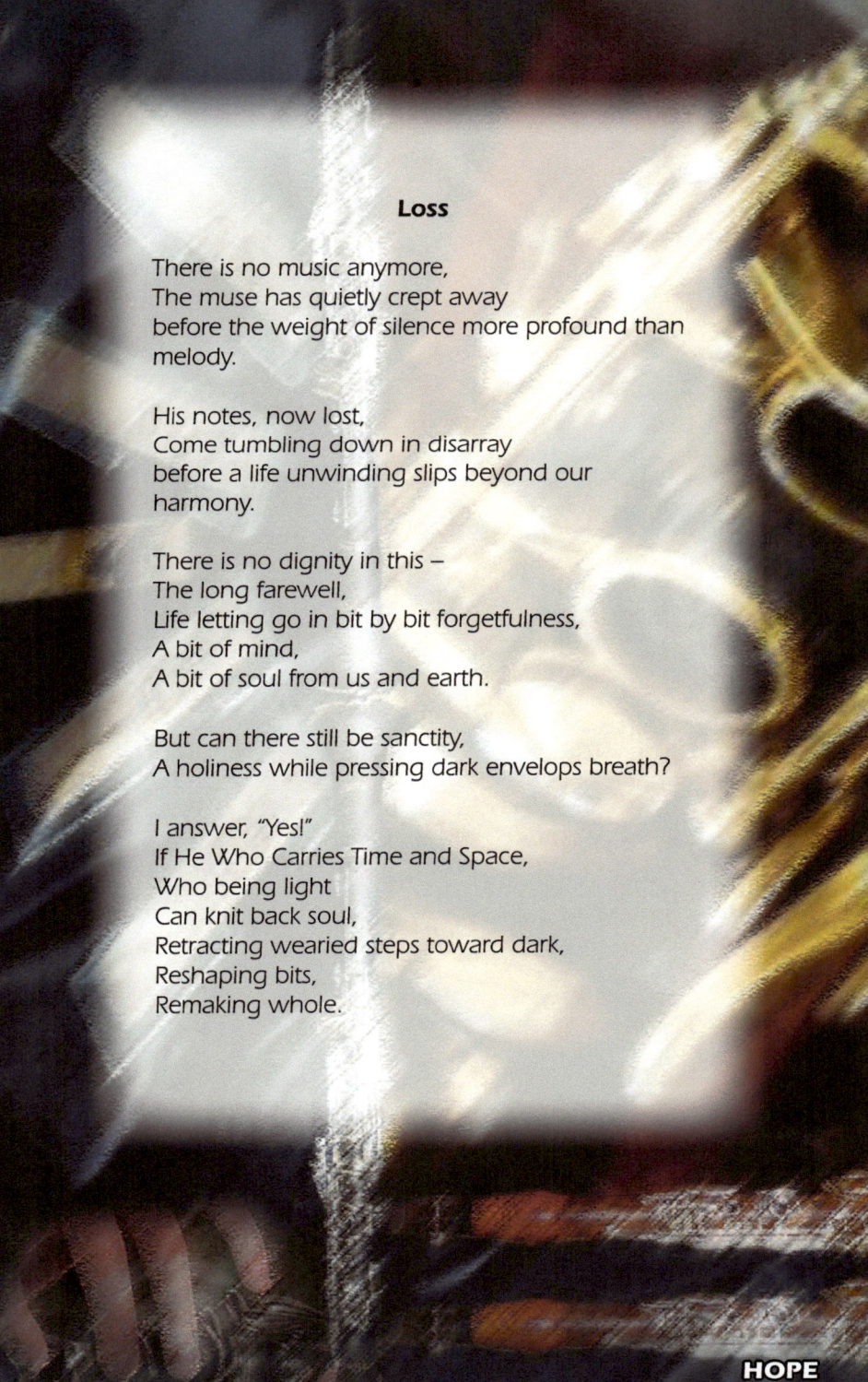

Loss

There is no music anymore,
The muse has quietly crept away
before the weight of silence more profound than melody.

His notes, now lost,
Come tumbling down in disarray
before a life unwinding slips beyond our harmony.

There is no dignity in this –
The long farewell,
Life letting go in bit by bit forgetfulness,
A bit of mind,
A bit of soul from us and earth.

But can there still be sanctity,
A holiness while pressing dark envelops breath?

I answer, "Yes!"
If He Who Carries Time and Space,
Who being light
Can knit back soul,
Retracting wearied steps toward dark,
Reshaping bits,
Remaking whole.

HOPE

Air Weighs

I can not breathe.
I am reminded of my father's labored breath,
His daily battle
Fighting endings,
Air forgotten,
Suffocation closing in
On man and death.

He didn't plan to give an inch,
He had decided not to go.
Instead he wrestled truth,
Pretending morphine drips
were only preludes to another course,
A grand adventure,
Always mending,
Breath-relenting pain
begetting future growth.

And we all watched reality take air away,
Loss by loss,
Hour by hour,
The obvious escaping him,
denial dripping out of bottles,
Drop by drop,
A soul syringed to counter pain,
and contradict with true disdain
the very thought of consequence,
of Providence and Deity.

So hard to watch,
So hard to lose.
Both father,
daughter,
unprepared
for death's inevitability.

(Where was the eagerness to go?
The Grand Adventure
waiting for a treasured son?

How could he hold and grasp
too tight this finite shell
that could not even carry air?
Where was his hope of heaven there?)

Here on the earth is what we know,
And so we care too much for friends,
for families,
for tangibles,
for memories.
God-given breath
is what we hold,
A vain control,
Our fragile Lilliputian gains
a brief exhale
before true wonders
blow away the shadowed veil,
Revealing Christ's infinity.

I wish my father could have faced
the course ahead,
from start to end,
And walked,
embracing better breaths
than those he chased.
(The Ph.D., his fading pride),
Leftovers from another time
so soon denied,
Where piety and intellect no longer mark
the face of faith.

So hard to gain,
So hard to lose,
So hard to let the Father choose.
So hard to wait,
So hard to breathe,
So hard to chase eternity.

HOPE

My Father's Last Days

One imperfect heart
gave an imperfect heart a hug.

Such hearts can never weight their world
with proper words,
or
carry love's hyperbole.

But still the snatched and scattered thoughts,
The caring deeds,
Were carefully and firmly pasted tight
by history and memories,
by hidden molding hands of Grace
so tenderly replacing
faulty parts with holy space.

He cried,
And then apologized.
But a daughter's heart accepts the tears.
(They are more kin to her than him,
And how could love not turn them into tender care,
Or more desire fellowship.)

She wanted words he could not share,
He gave her pride and rambling morphine diatribe,
All jumbled,
Existential language clouding air.

She asked for truth
And that he could not keep away,
The truth of death,
Of frailty,
Of battles fought and lost for oxygen and sanity.

He asked for hymns,
And here the hands of Grace re-shaped remaining flesh –
A heart set free to enter Christ's eternity.

And yet imperfect hearts remained,
Bereft
This daughter's struggling heart was left
for future days.

It did not seem to her
when morphine lisped,
When hospice overshadowed life
That hugs were there.

Yet looking back,
One fatherly imperfect heart,
And one imperfect daughter met together
on the fields of battle,
Each one fighting their own way,
Both wearied by a wasting foe,
Where bits and snatches,
Songs and deeds
(all love unspoken)
gathered by the God of Love,
Were shaped by Grace to make a hug.

HOPE

Isaiah 30:20-21

And though the Lord give you the bread of adversity and the water of affliction, yet your Teacher will not hide himself anymore, but your eyes shall see your Teacher. And your ears shall hear a word behind you, saying, "This is the way, walk in it," when you turn to the right or when you turn to the left.

Psalm 62: 1-2, 5-8

For God alone my soul waits in silence; from him comes my salvation. He only is my rock and my salvation, my fortress; I shall not be greatly shaken.

For God alone, O my soul, wait in silence, for my hope is from him. He only is my rock and my salvation, my fortress; I shall not be shaken. On God rests my salvation and my glory; my mighty rock, my refuge is God.

Trust in him at all times, O people; pour out your heart before him; God is a refuge for us.

Psalm 63:1-4

O God, you are my God; earnestly I seek you; my soul thirsts for you; my flesh faints for you, as in a dry and weary land where there is no water. So I have looked upon you in the sanctuary, beholding your power and glory. Because your steadfast love is better than life, my lips will praise you. So I will bless you as long as I live; in your name I will lift up my hands.

Psalm 116:1-15

I love the L ORD, because he has heard my voice and my pleas for mercy. Because he inclined his ear to me, therefore I will call on him as long as I live. The snares of death encompassed me; the pangs of Sheol laid hold on me; I suffered distress and anguish.

Then I called on the name of the L ORD: "O L ORD, I pray, deliver my soul!" Gracious is the L ORD, and righteous; our God is merciful. The L ORD preserves the simple; when I was brought low, he saved me. Return, O my soul, to your rest; for the L ORD has dealt bountifully with you.

For you have delivered my soul from death, my eyes from tears, my feet from stumbling; I will walk before the L ORD in the land of the living. I believed, even when I spoke, "I am greatly afflicted"; I said in my alarm, "All mankind are liars."

What shall I render to the L ORD for all his benefits to me? I will lift up the cup of salvation and call on the name of the L ORD, I will pay my vows to the L ORD in the presence of all his people.

HOPE

Tin Man

Let him be six
(like A.A. Milne),
Be gloriously six forever and ever.

(I had expected aged perfection,
A paragon of spiritual life.
It seems I half-expected god).

But there he lay,
A man of tin,
A human being just like me,
A son In Christ,
Yet burdened by imperfect thought,
By weaknesses,
his hesitations tumbling in
while cancer swallowed eager son
and stumbling steps replaced
a confidence in grace
once borne by arms
that carried me,
A life displayed before a child.

But I no longer am a child.
I am instead a woman
aged by righteous pain.
Also, like him, a son In Christ,
Also, like him, all molded tin.
And I begin to understand
that when the worst of sin descends,
when life's calamity
re-bends my tinny soul to shapes grotesque,
when finitudes demanding flaws
choose imperfections over best
and hearts are severed –
Also, like him, I would be six.

Now looking back,
where time has made
a gentle space for second thoughts,
I think this time,
"Let him be six,"
(like A.A. Milne),
"Let him be six forever and ever."

In the Trenches

We,
All poised for his last battle,
Fight,
Still hope,
Still walk the treacherous road together
Down
To breach the valley floor.

We are his warriors,
Battle-weary,
Praying for a victory,
A world beyond this cloying dark,
This final front,
A sanctuary built of light,
Where battles cease,
And holy warriors now released
from arms and terrors,
Gladly join their Savior's feast.

We celebrate as Morning
gathers battered hearts,
And wounds (still fresh),
Are not forgotten,
Tended,
Touched by healing Blood.

And scars remaining only shout
Of tendered Love,
Of remedies,
Of Life,
Of Joy,
And glorious Peace.

Psalm 18: 28-29

For it is you who light my lamp; the L\ORD my God lightens my darkness. For by you I can run against a troop, and by my God I can leap over a wall.

HOPE

Last Rites

Before I stroke a face of stone,
Once more
I place my earth-bound hand
inside of yours.
We,
Side by side,
devour air.
All silence,
No more need to share,
Or ponder weakness
withering ancient skin
on trembling bone.

I see your struggle to escape
A fading light.
Your body, wasting,
Hesitates
between two worlds,
Between Awaking and the night
that hovers here.

I tell you, "Go. Be whole,
be free."
And as I sing doxology,
Your hand leaves mine,
And eagerly,
Like sons who reach
to grasp and hold their fathers' hand,
You reach for His,
And so disband our company.
But gain instead
He who has always waited near.

I stand alone on holy ground.
You touch and know eternity.

Reflections

Did I see Christ
in the middle of Sam?
Could I learn grace
from a father of earth?
These sacred sights in memory,
Of a dad's delight in Scripture's Words,
and of his reverence for God –
Such heart's devotion's reverie
reflecting Christ's true love for me,
Became in time,
A testament of praise
before the One he served and prayed,
his breath and hymn
for all his days.

Sometimes Sam stood
in the middle of Christ.
And these sights also sculpted self.
The brilliant bright hyperbole
of pride's parade,
The grand desire to
conquer any accolade with greater gifts,
And garner visions both in life,
in work,
and church.

And yet, these bends
to alter God's determined Good,
Were met by Grace,
By humbling circumstance
that circumvented human could
for Greatest Should.

Did I see Christ
in the middle of Sam?
I say, I did.
And in this,
Sam has fathered me,
And by a life
held firm to Grace,
He touched my walk's eternity.

HOPE

I Corinthians 15:51-58

Behold! I tell you a mystery. We shall not all sleep, but we shall all be changed, in a moment, in the twinkling of an eye, at the last trumpet. For the trumpet will sound, and the dead will be raised imperishable, and we shall be changed. For this perishable body must put on the imperishable, and this mortal body must put on immortality. When the perishable puts on the imperishable, and the mortal puts on immortality, then shall come to pass the saying that is written: "Death is swallowed up in victory. O death, where is your victory? O death, where is your sting?" The sting of death is sin, and the power of sin is the law. But thanks be to God, who gives us the victory through our Lord Jesus Christ. Therefore, my beloved brothers, be steadfast, immovable, always abounding in the work of the Lord, knowing that in the Lord your labor is not in vain.

She Had No Hair

She had no hair,
But even then her face still shone.
And when the shadows literally
flashed across her face and seemed to fade her into
furniture that dressed her frame's eternity,
she still was her,
still feisty there,
a life expressing limited, yet relentless energy
that threatened cancer's raging throne.

Who but God could take
This ugly Rule
And make the shadows bow
To smiles I saw on Sheila's face?

I need to keep remembering
that there is always hope.
That Cancer cannot ever swallow
Heaven's grace,
Nor lay a funeral wreath
on one whom Jesus loves and owns.
For all the dark that death inflicts,
(For now, a casket full of dust),
Is ne'er as great as promises we've yet to taste,
Where even dirt and grass cannot
defend decay,
Nor this world's reigning rights prevent
The Sovereign Light Himself
from rising underneath.

HOPE

In Memory of Sheila

Psalm 31:14-15a But I trust in you, O Lord; I say, "You are my God." My times are in your hand.

Walk in the sun,
Run in the day,
Breathe the rustling air
whose warming thrills the heart,
and kisses face.
Remember moments being six,
where laughing greets a summer morn,
And smell the whiff of heaven's grace.

The body tires and bears
the scars of life and age.
It sometimes seems
that even souls are old,
And coldness creeps like wasting shadows
on an empty stage.

But Christ delights in aging souls,
And gathers such to fill His home.
Remaking ancient into ageless,
He reclaims our fading hopes.
He who nailed our death and sorrows,
battered skin adorning Cross,
Was swallowed up in resurrection,
Age upended,
Death's undoing,
"no more days" became tomorrows
Re-Creation conquering loss.

So walk in the sun,
Run in the day,
Breathe the rustling air
whose warming thrills the heart,
and kisses face.
Remember moments being six,
Where laughing greets a summer morn,
And smell the whiff of heaven's grace.

LIVING BY GRACE THROUGH LOSS

GRACE

Holy Love

Like Paul,
We all are chained to Holy pain,
Made prisoners of Gospel's love
through instruments that none would own -

a kidney stone,
a spouse's death,
a cruel loss,
a "cross to bear."

We cry aloud our heart's despair,
Forgetting
Only sons are loved this much,
Only sons of heavenly care.

The Heidelberg Catechism, Question 1*

Q. What is thy only comfort in life and in death?

A. That I with body and soul, both in life and in death, and not my own, but belong unto my faithful Savior, Jesus Christ; who, with his precious blood, has fully satisfied for all my sins, and delivered me from all the power of the devil; as so preserves me that without the will of my heavenly Father, not a hair can fall from my head; yea, that all things must be subservient to my salvation, and therefore, by his Holy Spirit, He also assures me of eternal life, and makes me sincerely willing and ready, henceforth, to live unto him.

* Reprinted with permission from The Heidelberg Catechism Translation (c) 1969,
Christian Reformed Church of North America.

Psalm 146:3-6

Put not your trust in princes, in a son of man, in whom there is no salvation. When his breath departs, he returns to the earth; on that very day his plans perish. Blessed is he whose help is the God of Jacob, whose hope is in the L<small>ORD</small> his God, who made heaven and earth, the sea, and all that is in them, who keeps faith forever.

Psalm 61:1-2

Hear my cry, O God, listen to my prayer; from the end of the earth I call to you when my heart is faint. Lead me to the rock that is higher than I.

GRACE

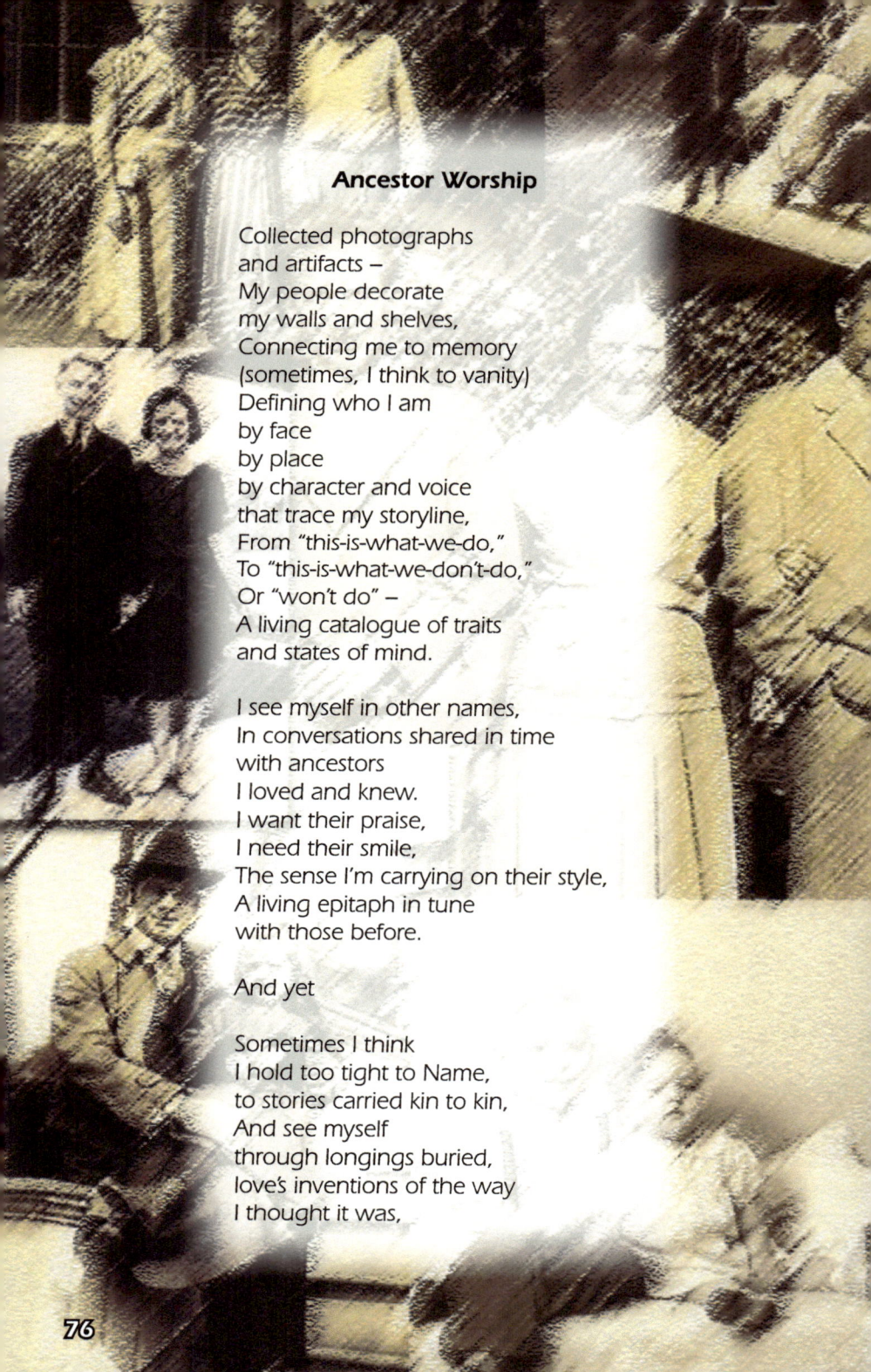

Ancestor Worship

Collected photographs
and artifacts –
My people decorate
my walls and shelves,
Connecting me to memory
(sometimes, I think to vanity)
Defining who I am
by face
by place
by character and voice
that trace my storyline,
From "this-is-what-we-do,"
To "this-is-what-we-don't-do,"
Or "won't do" –
A living catalogue of traits
and states of mind.

I see myself in other names,
In conversations shared in time
with ancestors
I loved and knew.
I want their praise,
I need their smile,
The sense I'm carrying on their style,
A living epitaph in tune
with those before.

And yet

Sometimes I think
I hold too tight to Name,
to stories carried kin to kin,
And see myself
through longings buried,
love's inventions of the way
I thought it was,

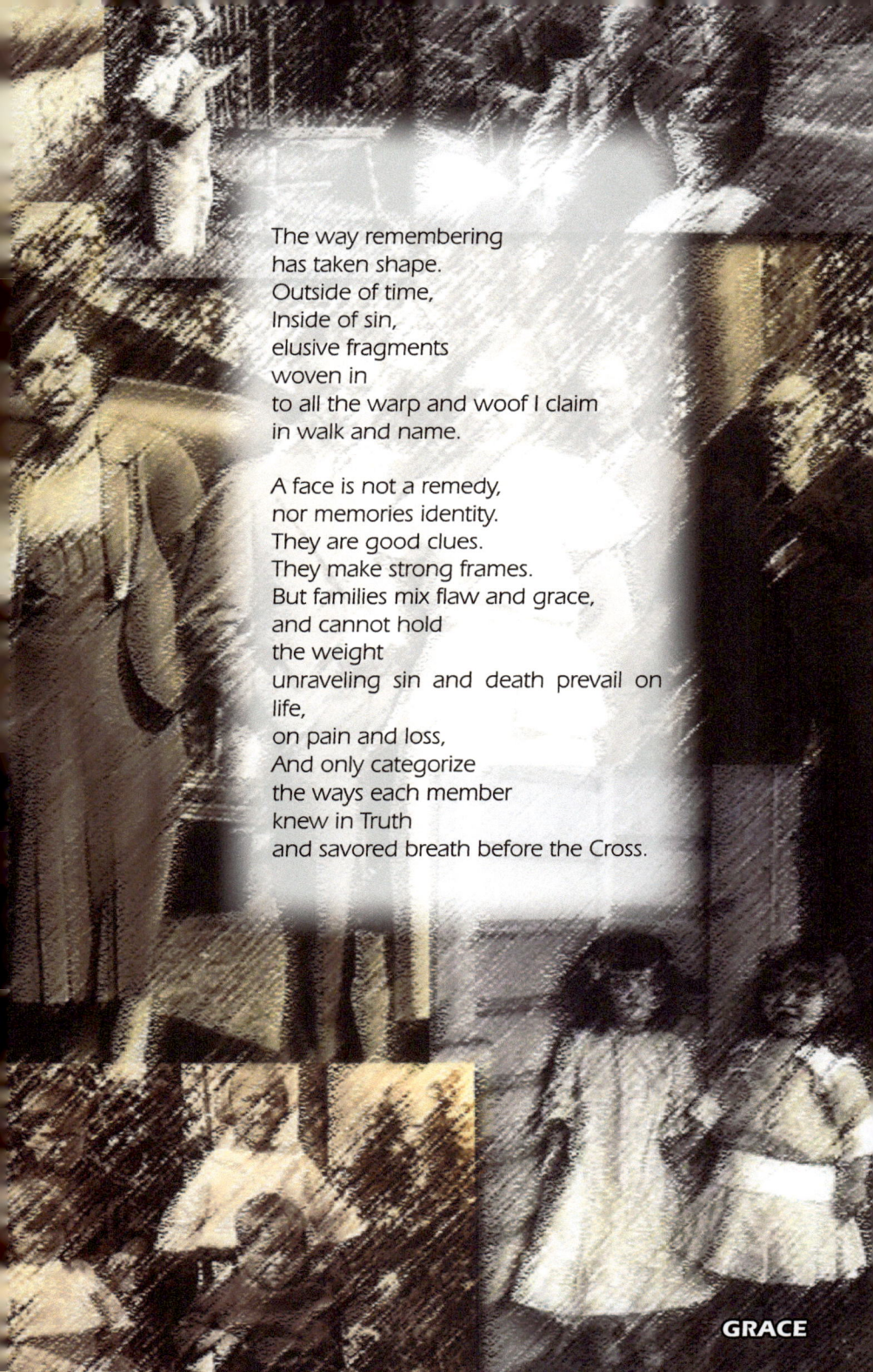

The way remembering
has taken shape.
Outside of time,
Inside of sin,
elusive fragments
woven in
to all the warp and woof I claim
in walk and name.

A face is not a remedy,
nor memories identity.
They are good clues.
They make strong frames.
But families mix flaw and grace,
and cannot hold
the weight
unraveling sin and death prevail on life,
on pain and loss,
And only categorize
the ways each member
knew in Truth
and savored breath before the Cross.

GRACE

Shadows

There they are –
Black and white,
Old photos
capturing single moments,
Smiles suspended,
Light and shadows
shaping pasts
without explaining history,
or comprehending what would come.

Just little boys on tricycles
with eager eyes,
And little girls in matching dresses,
Wistfully addressing us,
Our face to theirs,
Our sorrows' hidden accidents
from these remembered memories.
Stilled hearts
Untouched by fraying life,
Our finitude in seconds caught,
Like pushing pause on times unending,
Days unbending,
Endless rush.

What happened to the little boy
who favored red, and flannel shirts,
Who much preferred heroic jumps
to taking stairs?

What happened to the woman-child,
One moment jump ropes everywhere,
The next a dress of dreams
and princess expectations overpowering dirt?

We can't go back.

Flat film can only hold
a passing thought,
And underline to
every age how much
our lives are fading wind.

What is,
Is WAS,
Already making history a ruthless power
where even breathing
can't rescind
a moving clock,
But only push us further in
To human past,
To new old photos
Documenting
What was once our children's hour.

But finitude
Is not our end in Holy Writ,
Nor sentimental pictures
pledging immortality,
Our final place.

That stark reminder,
Frailty,
Is second skin,
And also Jesus' pressure point
to draw us into fellowship
and Sacred trust.

For who, but Vast Eternity,
Intruding into time and space
Could understand our elements,
Our constant grasp
for permanence.

He Re-creates
our image,
healing faces,
bodies,
marred and blurred,
by restless sin.
He sacrifices
Blood for blood,
His Death for death,
His saving Wind,
New Breath revives
our souls to IS.

GRACE

Ownership

I never really owned myself.
It seems a thoughtless dream
when I am dealing with a God who raises from the dead.
But here I am,
All human,
Planning out my own desires,
my own applause,
expecting somehow,
earnestness,
sincerity, could balance human frailty with
awesome God.

Like Abraham I argue from my little world –
Will you save ten?
Ten power realms to call my own?
Or maybe five – you run the rest.
Okay, just one –
Massaging ego,
bruised and helplessly alone.
Dear God, do I own anything??

And He says, "No. I own it all.
Before I called Creation's light,
Before the Flood,
Before a single Israelite knew altar blood,
Before a king or prophet stood,
Before the Gentiles even looked, or wanted Good,
I wrote your name into my book,
I chose your life.
And Jesus signed His name in blood across your page.
When judgment called, He took your place.
Your life is mine.
My heart is yours.
You are my son eternally,
You are the heir of righteousness, of love, of grace."

And so you see,
I never really owned me.

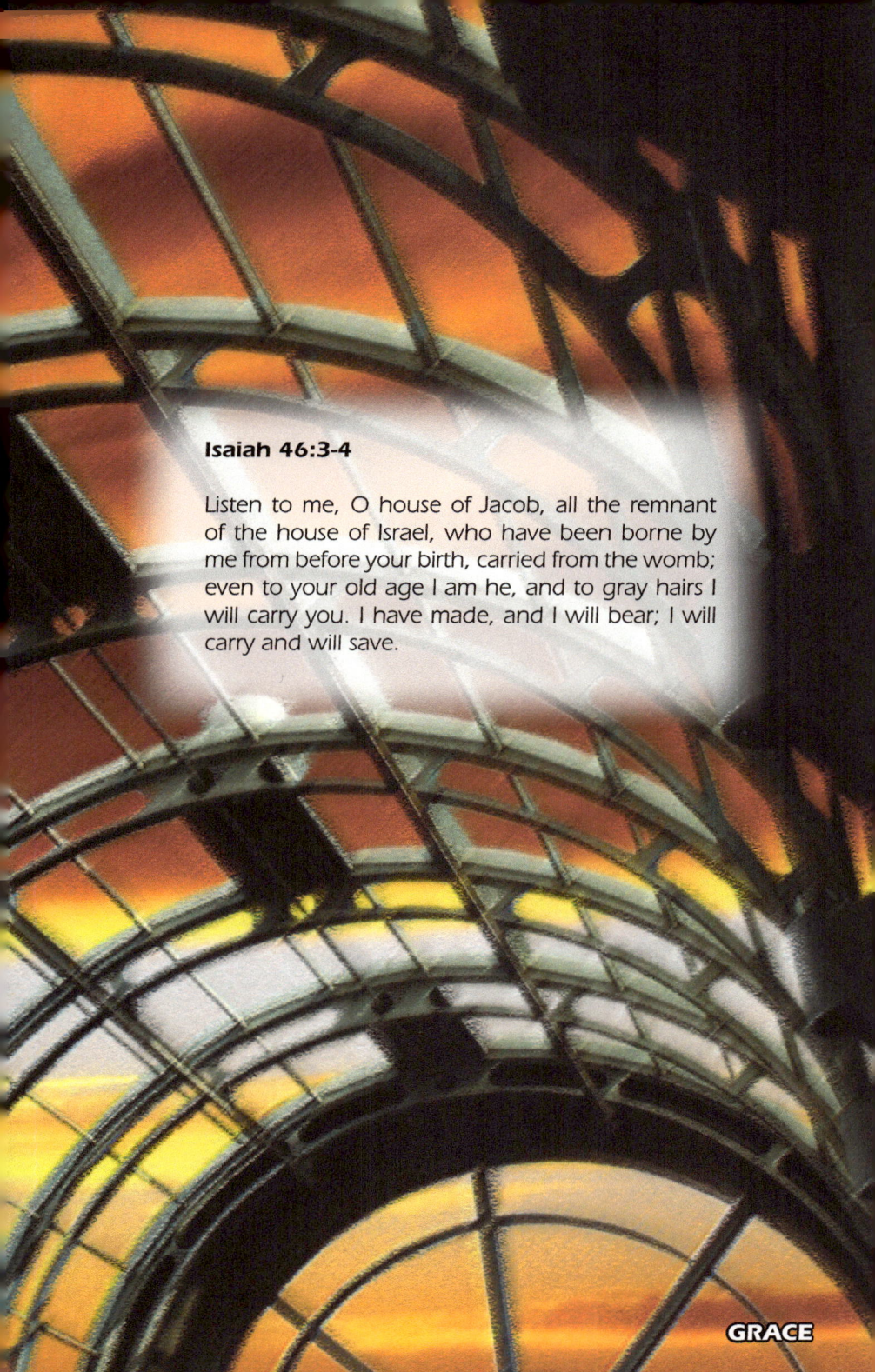

Isaiah 46:3-4

Listen to me, O house of Jacob, all the remnant of the house of Israel, who have been borne by me from before your birth, carried from the womb; even to your old age I am he, and to gray hairs I will carry you. I have made, and I will bear; I will carry and will save.

Potter's Work

Isaiah 64:8 But now, O L*ORD*, you are our Father; we are the clay, and you are our potter; we are all the work of your hand.

He uses broken pots for noble works.
Ewers, cracked and chipped by constant use,
Mixing bowls and jugs,
and faded flowerpots,
All stained and grayed by time's abuse.

Sometimes I wonder
why this lump of clay
has gotten perks so undeserved?
But that's just it –
No pottery is given say,
No pottery itself can choose.

The Potter shapes containers for His needs,
and lovingly arranges clay to follow suit.

And then,
Amazingly,
He does not toss away a damaged piece,
But finds another use,
New ways for potter's clay,
New honored deeds.

*Heidelberg Catechism, Question 27

Q. What dost thou mean by the providence of God?

A. The almighty and everwhere present power of God; whereby, as it were by his hand, he upholds and governs heaven, earth, and all creatures; so that herbs and grass, rain and drought, fruitful and barren years, meat and drink, health and sickness, riches and poverty, yea, and all things come, not by chance, but by His fatherly hand.

*Heidelberg Catechism, Question 28

Q. What advantage is it to us to know that God has created, and by his providence does still uphold all things?

A. That we may be patient in adversity; thankful in prosperity; and that in all things, which may hereafter befall us, we place our firm trust in our faithful God and Father, that nothing shall separate us from his love; since all creatures are so in his hand, that without his will they cannot so much as move.

Romans 8:38-39

For I am sure that neither death nor life, nor angels nor rulers, nor things present nor things to come, nor powers, nor height nor depth, nor anything else in all creation, will be able to separate us from the love of God in Christ Jesus our Lord.

* Reprinted with permission from The Heidelberg Catechism Translation (c) 1969,
  Christian Reformed Church of North America.

GRACE

Gardening

He sent a letter through His friends,
And when I read it
all His words were buried deep,
Like weighted seeds,
Protected from the rocky path,
More strongly rooted
than the weeds soon springing up,
(This jumbled hedge
Of fearful dreads and anxious parts),
Cruel vines,
Their leafy edges marking shadows
In the Light,
And choking hope from promises and trusting
thoughts.

But His words sprinkled in a soil of righteous
blood,
And daily tended
by the Gardener's faithful toil,
Will raise in me
A harvest of courageous deeds,
A life devoted to the One
Who is the Word,
Who is the Letter written
carefully in nails and wood upon my heart.

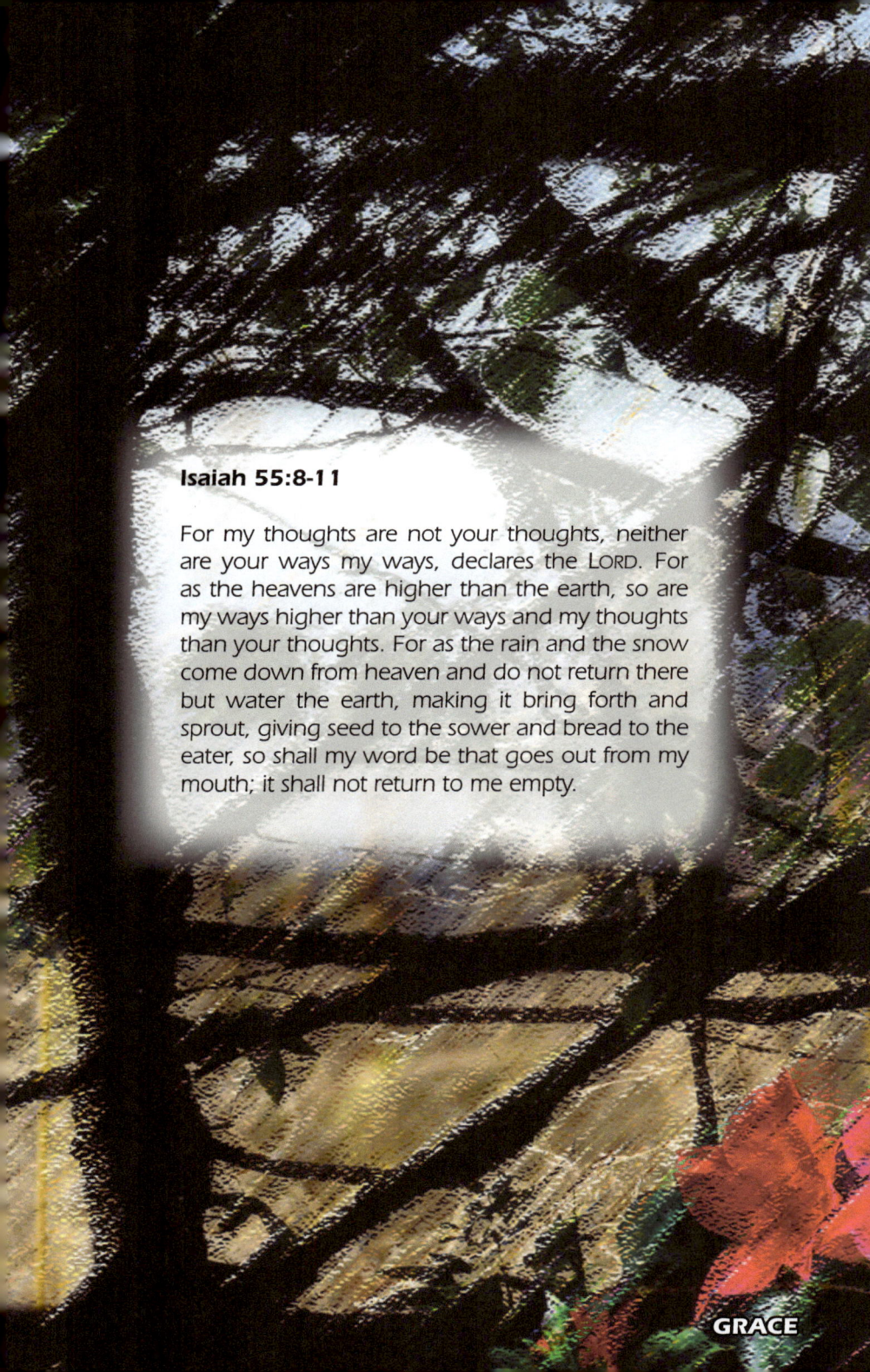

Isaiah 55:8-11

For my thoughts are not your thoughts, neither are your ways my ways, declares the Lord. For as the heavens are higher than the earth, so are my ways higher than your ways and my thoughts than your thoughts. For as the rain and the snow come down from heaven and do not return there but water the earth, making it bring forth and sprout, giving seed to the sower and bread to the eater, so shall my word be that goes out from my mouth; it shall not return to me empty.

GRACE

Ephesians 1:16-23

I do not cease to give thanks for you, remembering you in my prayers, that the God of our Lord Jesus Christ, the Father of glory, may give you a spirit of wisdom and of revelation in the knowledge of him, having the eyes of your hearts enlightened, that you may know what is the hope to which he has called you, what are the riches of his glorious inheritance in the saints, and what is the immeasurable greatness of his power toward us who believe, according to the working of his great might that he worked in Christ when he raised him from the dead and seated him at his right hand in the heavenly places, far above all rule and authority and power and dominion, and above every name that is named, not only in this age but also in the one to come. And he put all things under his feet and gave him as head over all things to the church, which is his body, the fullness of him who fills all in all.

Prisons of the Heart

When you're in prison,
All you see is the bars,
Alone,
Cut off,
'til fear of alienation scars
deep wounds and doubts
in righteous trust.

And then you notice
you're still alive,
Still moving around.
The place is small (it may be a box),
But you can breathe,
and think,
and pray.

And suddenly (like Paul and Silas locked in stocks),
You hear Christ's voice,
His strength stands tall,
And you can sing.

And energies like earthquakes
rock complacencies,
and lift the roof off smothered hope.

You're still in prison,
But now you cope.
The room still small,
But light devours what once was dark,
The roof is off,
And night is pierced
in a million dots by glorious stars.

GRACE

Out of Egypt

How long have I believed in Egypt?
Like Abraham, I chose the south,
to take that road,
to walk alone.
Like Jacob, begging men for grain,
(If a child asks for bread, would He give her a stone?)
I longed like Israel for leeks,
forgetting Egypt's sweat and pain,
when manna overflowed like snow,
and fed a hunger I disdained.

Why build my bricks without the straw?
Why labor on these rooms of mud?
When Christ has already passed over,
and I am living under blood?

I find, it's time to leave the Nile,
neglect my pyramids of sand,
To take my weary wander north,
beyond Negev,
and step into the Promised Land,
Where I like Joseph carry Jacob,
Homeward heart comes back
To Mamre,
Back to promises of old,
Like Joshua I bury sorrows,
Ancient bones in Shechem's soil.

Messiah whispers, "Follow me,"
and I let go of Egypt's toil.
Messiah beckons,
I will follow,
Out of Egypt
into Canaan Recreated,
into Christ's eternal home.

Ebenezer

I am a life of standing stones.
"Thus far," I say,
Like ancient Samuel did before,
"The LORD has helped."

Yet I make war on waiting rooms,
Those places in-between
God's "yes" and "no"
where anxious pacing
wears away the walls and floors
of limitations boxing trust
and testing soul.

Where I want doors,
He whispers, "wait,"
And I must linger in the dust
of daily care,
all energies left unresolved,
Like Jacob, wrestling
with the One who put him there.

And yet,
Like Jacob,
Hanging on, not letting go,
I know this place is also rest,
Where I must wait
and count the stones
that saved my life.
The spaces God has given Best,
have been my Good
when troubled heart
has tested bones and worried blood.

His place, still safe,
Still better for a wrestling heart,
And He reminds of other days,
My story filled with rescues
heaped like Ebenezer's marking grace,
an endless store.

"Thus far," I say,
Like ancient Samuel did before,
"The LORD has helped."

GRACE

Blessed are the Poor in Spirit

So here it is, my rescue,
You the God Who Sees,
You who chased me down
through deserts of the soul,
And did not let my wander
give me name,
but made me free.

I could have been a Hagar child,
Another daughter lost
to my own slavery.
But you decided otherwise,
And most profound,
You chose before
divine imagination made a world.

"The Lord Will Provide," he said.
My ancient father trusted you
to raise the dead,
to overcome the Great Impossibility.

How can I not trust as well
on this,
The ground I stand,
When fearing threatens infertility
of faith and rest?
And I am hurled from prideful self-sufficiency
to restless, weary poverty,
dependence borrowing anxious dread.

And then, I see this poverty
For what it is,
My rescue
wrapped in packages of fear.
Daily opportunities
to run to Him,
To trust like Abraham before,
To wait in expectation of
His glorious grace
attached to death,
The nailing of anxiety upon the Cross.
The slow and painful letting go
of Who Is Scared
for one who finds Peniel
where I see Jesus face to face.

GRACE

My Wilderness

This world delights in panic mode.
It sends its seekers
on patrol to field a fear,
To elevate adrenaline
until we breathe its tensions in,
And seal the dread,
This fragile universe exhales among the dead –
Sound bites at five,
Opinions ratified at ten.
They say someday the world will end.

And so it will.

I fight the tether of these fears,
I feel its fingers reaching in,
I cannot carry life's estate upon my back.
I have a frail and this-world skin.
I cannot shoulder earthly sin
Or shatter all the enemies
that misery sends.

And yet,
Sometimes I lift a corner off
This quaking world,
and try to shoulder God's domain,
The God who made me, head to toe,
Who breathes in me my daily breath,
The God who guides my stumbling feet
Around the traps that lead to death.

I live the wilderness of fights.
The testing ground for learning trust.
It doesn't do
to think my will,
My human will might pave a way.
Men always fail.
They cannot save,
Man's mercies cannot comprehend
What sin requires,
Or end the helplessness that
strains the human heart
With smoke and fires.

And so I trust,
And I, too, fail.
Some days are lost,
And I am hurled by energies
That labor air.
Reminding me
I wasn't meant to bear this world.

Some days I live from hour to hour,
A seeker of God's greater rest,
His perfect Grace
A shelter in my time's unknown,
A God more powerful than Fates,
His faithful Providence designed,
A God more powerful than wealth
Or politics could redefine,
God more electrical and bright than technological displays,
More deeply real in pure delights than grand imagination's play.

There always will be urgent fears,
A steady siren call
Of crisis
calling in life's marketplace,
Rebellion aching for a taste of war,
Like ancient echoes gone before.

But here I stand –
Securely caught in Sovereign Love,
My heart remains,
My name already spoken for
In saving blood,
And Christ is also on patrol,
In strength and patience
Gathering people just like me
From restlessness,
The undertow of discontent
He took alone, unraveling shame's eternity.

And here I stand –
Awaiting Promise yet to be,
When Christ Himself will
come upending Adam's curse,
with Re-Creation's Holy mend.
And in that Day, I bury fear,
Forever free.
And then, I know this world will end.

GRACE

A Mighty Fortress Is Our God
Martin Luther, 1529

A mighty fortress is our God, a bulwark never failing;
Our helper he amid the flood of mortal ills prevailing.
For still our ancient foe
doth seek to work us woe;
his craft and power are great;
And armed with cruel hate, on earth is not his equal.

Did we in our own strength confide,
our striving would be losing;
Were not the right man on our side,
the man of God's own choosing.
Dost ask who that may be?
Christ Jesus it is he,
Lord Sabaoth his name,
From age to age the same, and he must win the battle.

And though this world, with devils filled,
should threaten to undo us,
We will not fear for God hath willed his truth
to triumph through us.
The prince of darkness grim,
We tremble not for him;
His rage we can endure,
For lo! His doom is sure. One little word shall fell him.

That Word above all earthly pow'rs,
no thanks to them, abideth;
The Spirit and the gifts are ours
through him who with us sideth.
Let goods and kindred go,
This mortal life also;
The body they may kill:
God's truth abideth still; His kingdom is forever.

Psalm 59:16-17

But I will sing of your strength; I will sing aloud of your steadfast love in the morning. For you have been to me a fortress and a refuge in the day of my distress. O my Strength, I will sing praises to you, for you, O God, are my fortress, the God who shows me steadfast love.

Refiner's Fire

There is no Ph.D. in Christ,
No need to prove ourselves complete.
No need to worry
Pride and Selfishness
will find a settled seat,
like squatters,
grazing mercilessly away
on fields of high sincerity,
on thousand-acre words and boasts
defining fearful hearts
alone,
desiring always to be free.

Instead,

There is a Head.
Himself declaring, "Follow me."
Himself the settled one,
The Harvester
devouring useless grass and withered fields,
Declaring enmity
Between our Pride and us,
Between our selfish hearts and sin.
Himself refining,
Burning off the misery
that binds our fragile souls to death.

And we,
Once fearing to be found
imperfect,
Now discover worries snatched away.
And we are left no more alone.
No less ourselves.
In Him complete.
No need to prove our Ph.D.

GRACE

Unfinished Friends

I have a friend,
At least a friendly "hi" in church,
Or accidental meetings at the store,
Where we exchange bland pleasantries,
But never,
ever,
Bandage sores
that peel like scabs each time we pass
or intersect.

Instead some superficial thoughts,
Like blankets,
Smother tensions bubbling underneath,
Unfinished thoughts
that leave the heart unsatisfied,
And cannot find
A bridge
Between two friends,
Who could be walking,
working side by side.

There are instead
Two sinful hearts,
Two separate ways to see the world,
Euodia and Syntyche,
Both doing right,
Both serving for eternity,
Yet somehow separate,
Viewing from a different lens.

And I would love
to find the words to gentle space,
But such may never be our grace.

And so I rest my burdened self
On Jesus' arms,
And know,
She, too, is resting there,
Two restless hearts,
Both women
Waiting for a promised place,
A universe,
Not yet revealed,
Where we are free
to love and live in all our parts.

'Til then we wait,
Unfinished friends.

Under Construction

Some days I am amazed at God,
Who graciously
repairs the plaster,
Filling in the cracks and dents we make,
Relationships more grit than growth,
Where we are all
Sandpaper,
Opening wounds and vents
instead of soothing life's offense,
And covering over
multitudes of hurts with Holy Hope.

It seems,
Too often,
We forget the Architect and Builder
of our city walls is Christ.
Instead we bury mud and dust,
(with structures one time carved from enmity
and Lamech's boasts,
Poor cardboard houses,
Chicken-wired,
Nailed and taped
to earth's idolatry and ghosts.)

Yet now we own a heavenly home,
(Hard stones of Holy Sacrifice
all mortared by His blood),
And we are named
"Wall-Builders,"
Sacred workmen called
To join with Christ repairing lives,
and lifting eyes and hearts toward love.

I am not always building up,
And in my frailty,
My plaster cannot smooth away all tired tears.
But Christ is able,
Filling in around my feeble work,
Rebuilding hope from
sheets of tin and cardboard halls,
with stable Reconciliation's plastered walls.

GRACE

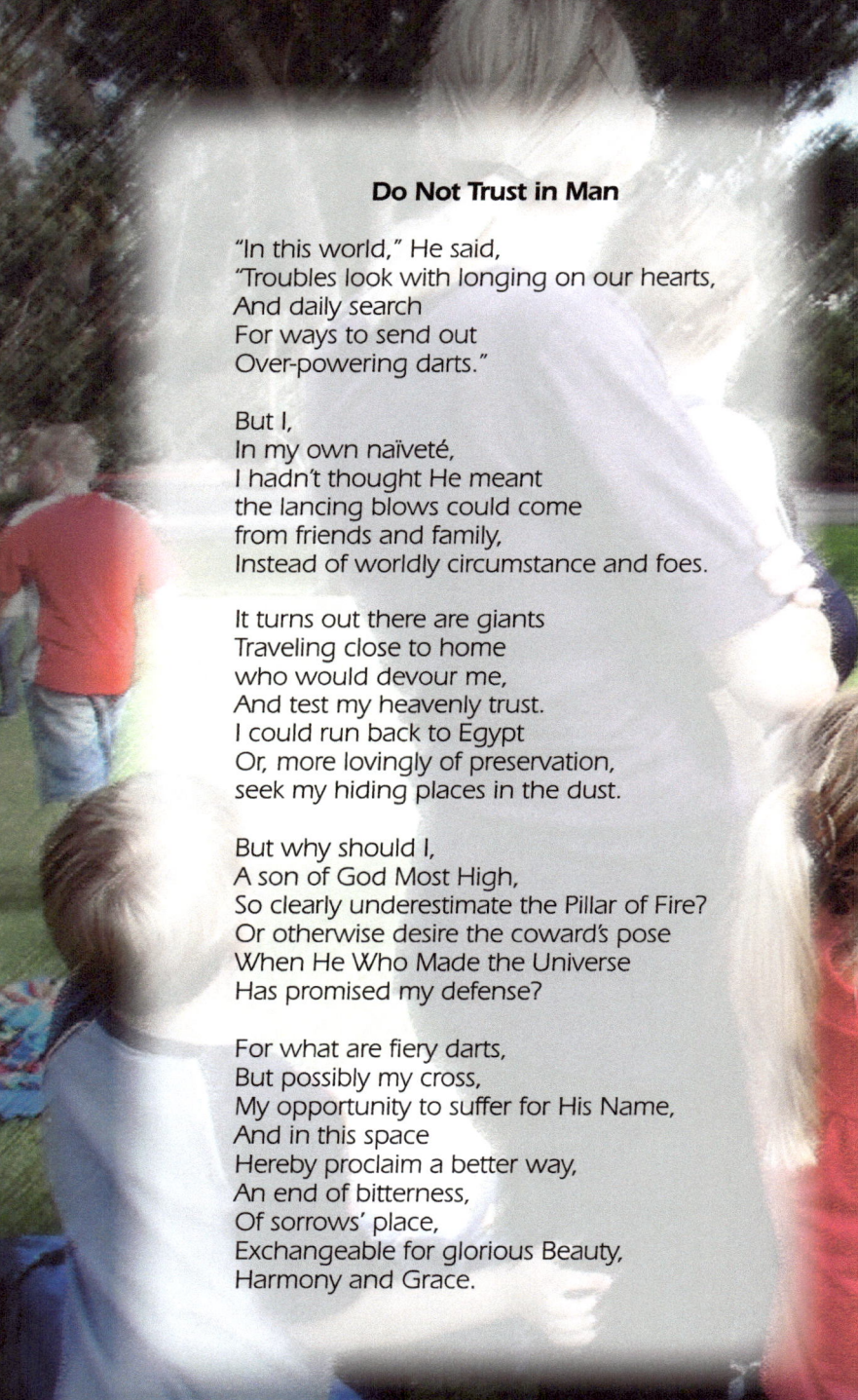

Do Not Trust in Man

"In this world," He said,
"Troubles look with longing on our hearts,
And daily search
For ways to send out
Over-powering darts."

But I,
In my own naïveté,
I hadn't thought He meant
the lancing blows could come
from friends and family,
Instead of worldly circumstance and foes.

It turns out there are giants
Traveling close to home
who would devour me,
And test my heavenly trust.
I could run back to Egypt
Or, more lovingly of preservation,
seek my hiding places in the dust.

But why should I,
A son of God Most High,
So clearly underestimate the Pillar of Fire?
Or otherwise desire the coward's pose
When He Who Made the Universe
Has promised my defense?

For what are fiery darts,
But possibly my cross,
My opportunity to suffer for His Name,
And in this space
Hereby proclaim a better way,
An end of bitterness,
Of sorrows' place,
Exchangeable for glorious Beauty,
Harmony and Grace.

100

THE DEATH OF LOSS AND THE BIRTH OF JOY

Because of Christ, hope is always peeking at the corners of life, lifting the edges of despair back to expose the light that is always underneath. It may be only a little light, but it is there, dogged and determined to show itself when we least expect, when there is the lowest possibility of hope, and in the most terrible suffering.

JOY

Take it Off!

Take it off!
Strip away the crumpled chrysalis that binds this life to earth.
Take it off!
Don't let me hold too tight to what I cannot keep.
Take it off!
And I, like Eustace, bear the pain to have the dragon swept away.
Take it off!
And let me fly to You.

In Memory of Baby Emily

Baby bird,
Lie in your nest,
And breathe the sleep
of endless rest.
You came in spring,
In spring you died,
And all the weeping willows cried
and bowed their backs to hug the earth,
And would not tickle early grass,
Or sing the wind to come and dance
because you left us in the night,
And would not stay
Before the dawn could warm the day,
Before the day could bring the light.

She is an eagle,
Soaring high above the crowds
of chattering birds.
She is an eagle,
Rushing, charging into sky,
A silhouette against the clouds.
She is an eagle,
Laughing, breaking up the wind
with rustling wings
that nudge the breeze
and brush away the silent air.
She is an eagle,
Floating on a sea of light
that wraps her,
Holds her poised in flight,
Beyond the glare that blocks my view,
And toward the heavens waiting there.

JOY

In Memory of Edie and Betty

Two women searched the Cross today,
Two souls who lay beneath the weight of ruthless life,
From Adam's poverty,
All wasting holy image.

Yet

The Cross descending consecrates,
And re-creates two toiling hearts.

The Rest begun.

Two lives transformed,
But still with outsides worn away,
Both mind and marrow
Helpless,
Suffering entropy.

They come to us
Disabled by the grip of light becoming gray,
Where once lay strength,
Now bits and pieces –
Paper aching bones and
Scattered memories delights.

Yet still these two,
These women (more than most) are two
who gave up what they could not hold,
To gain what they would never lose.

Like Tabithas laid out by grief in Sunday's best,
Their bodies stilled,
All conversation lost and cold,
Awaiting in an upstairs room
For One to come,
To draw out breath from death's repose,
From all the weeping widows bent before their earth.

Two women searched the Cross today,
And found instead
their resurrection from the dead.

Requiem for Nita

Too many years
Are drained away by dying's noise.
Too many words are
Wrenched
From hearts already kissed by heaven's voice.
And I,
Apart,
Can only watch, while wintered winds
drive breath from life.
And patient death makes love bereft.

I ask for peace,
When life,
(full speed)
Comes roaring up into my face –
A bellowing wind
that bruises hope and scatters grace.
I ask for grace,
When endless shadows swirl above.
(Their haunting voices echo pain)
A mocking wind
that snatches hope,
And empties love.
I ask for love,
And hear the Name commanding, "Peace!"
He stills the wind,
Rekindling hope
as raging sorrow finds release.

Gentle Morpheus,
Ease the pain,
'til sleep itself becomes the gate
Between who was
And He Who Is.
Don't let cocooning us
hold on to her whom Jesus loves.
Let soul depart,
And woman fly
to Jesus' heart,
Where death is gain.

JOY

She Has Arrived!

She has arrived!
And heaven smiles on constancy so bravely borne,
Endurance worn by tendered face
Still patiently avowing grace.
She has arrived!
And we,
Like shadows,
Hover near eternal beds
and view at last relentless death,
Its sadness seeping heart and bone.
"Too soon!" we cry,
Remembering the ageless days before disease,
Before the cancer bodied breath,
And we are left all Marthas pressed against the tomb
while Lazarus sleeps awaiting Life.
"No pain," we say,
Consoling us,
Embracing helplessly against our night.

Yet He, who raging stood between the dark and us,
Who cowered death,
Demanding Lazarus take breath and
weave again his soul to flesh –
This Warrior King devoured dark in His own blood,
And would not settle in the grave for man's decay,
But grasping immortality in endless hands,
He offered back (what Adam lost)
in glorious dress.
And Sheila,
Chosen from Before to be a daughter of the King,
To carry pain with heavenly grace –
This child no longer lies in dust,
But stands in glory at the feet of One Who Saves.
And she (no more a shade) reveals
What we will be when finite meets eternity.
No more in dark,
No more in pain,
No more the solitude of soul that empties peace.
So near the grave – Yet not in night.
She has Become.
And all our shadows fade away in glittering light.
She has Arrived!

In Memory of Sandra

Spring comes early here this year,
And Life,
Reviving,
Swiftly swallows winter's sleep in morning light,
In all the true and brightest blues that tune
awakening hearts for flight.

"Come away," the Morning whispers,
"Come away to wiser worlds.
Leave behind your night and shadows,
Find your day in time unfurled."

Spring comes early here this year,
And Life,
Renewing,
Wrests the heart from winter's arid cold and curse,
Forgetting frost at last is lost as living water
quenches thirst.

"Come away," the River beckons,
"Come away to sweeter streams.
Leave behind the taste of sorrow,
Only drink where Life redeems."

Spring comes early here this year,
And Life,
Rebuilding,
Gathers up the tattered snatch of broken branch,
Remaking glorious nest from winter's cast-offs,
Scrub becomes Creation's best.

"Come away," the Builder counters,
"Come away! Your room is done.
Leave behind your pilgrim status,
Enter in, my faithful one!"

And so she left us,
Leaving mother, daughter, wife,
She could not wait.
But who would hesitate when death
is swallowed up in Life?

JOY

Chrysalis

He's an old man leaning on yesterday's laurels,
He's a boy with a glimpse of eternity's feast.
Hands made of earth are reaching for heaven,
Feet made of clay are shuffling east.

One more day on this side of his birthday,
One more hour in time and space,
Soon to be breathing only Tomorrow,
Soon to Be only Love and Grace.

No more books to write and reason,
The Book of Life at last unsealed.
No more words for comprehending,
Now the Word Himself revealed.

No more marriage made in heaven,
He becomes the faithful bride.
No more earthly cares and worries,
Now that soul is satisfied.

Earthly harmony relenting,
Leaves the singer all alone.
New songs sung are never ending
as he stands before the Throne.

He's an old man changed in a moment of breathing,
He's a boy, he's a man held in sanctified light.
Hands made of Grace can no longer hold shadows,
Feet made of Love never walk into night.

In Memory of Glen

Sing for the son if you can.
Sing for the one who is dead.
Sing if you can,
If you cannot, listen.

Where can I stand when I no longer kiss his face,
Nor run a hand with easy grace on aching arms
too soon removed?
There are no hugs among the dead.

How can I stand when memories of what there was
(of happiness and joyful ease before disease)
Come hissing in like chilling wind,
Like wrapping dark to whisper thoughts
an aching heart would savor most?
There is no voice among the dead.

Sing for the son if you can.
Sing for the one who is dead.
Sing if you can,
If you cannot, listen.

But there is a Son who was and is,
Who danced the fragile line
between an endless state and seasoned time,
Who took our weathered form
and wore our crime to face our death.
There is a guilt among the dead.

For only He could carry man,
Could lift the burden of our death,
(our ponderous, pale fragility),
To shoulder dark we could not bear,
A hopeless debt,
Our enmity His agony,
'Til crushing grace unraveled night
and emptied all of our regret.
The morning dawns among the dead.

So death begins its backward run,
What's done at last becomes undone,
Unmade,
Our sorrows unbegun.
No longer death, no more the grave,
As sadness seized by piercing light
declares the end of soul-less night.

Sing for the Son if you can.
Sing for the One who was dead,
Sing for the One who is now alive!

So here I stand,
A traveler caught between two worlds,
In tendered grief, my feet on earth,
Yet eyes above to savor Grace
Revealed within an empty tomb.
He promises of Life to come
(my heart undone).
"Stand firm!" He says,
"Behold your King!"
The One who empties my distress,
Who peels mortality away like useless skin,
This One will raise Glen from the dead,
And wrap a body turned to dust in greater dress.

Sing for the son if you can.
Sing for the one who was dead.
Sing for One who is now alive!
Sing for the One!
Sing for the One!

JOY

Isaiah 25:6-8

On this mountain the LORD Almighty will prepare a feast of rich food for all peoples, a banquet of aged wine - the best of meats and the finest of wines. On this mountain he will destroy the shroud that enfolds all peoples, the sheet that covers all nations; he will swallow up death forever. The Sovereign LORD will wipe away the tears from all faces; he will remove the disgrace of his people from all the earth.

The LORD has spoken. (NIV)

Thoughts on Standing in a Graveyard

His ruthless friendship
Bore the weight of granite will,
(paralysis that buries soul)
No carelessness could topple rock,
Monuments to death's unknown.
But only Love,
Deliberate,
Braved human frame and frailty,
Dared mingle hope with suffering
'til death-defying holy laughter melted stone.

JOY

Rapture

Wind
Unwinds the clanging bells
Shouting in an unknown tongue,
Knocking hard against His house
Like wet clothes
Slapping on the line.

The ringing
Echoes in the air
Where people-stones in garden rows
No longer hear the rage of life
Nor silent death.

But listening to a different sound
Above the earth,
All wide awake,
They're changed from darkness into day,
Their bodies free
(this thought profound)
They have become
Beyond!

Dear Reader:

Jesus told His disciples, "In this world you will have trouble," (John 16:33)*, and my life, like yours, has been sometimes hammered by the pains of this world – grief, loss, physical limitation, and the disappointments that mark all our human relationships.

I have been a Christian since a young child, and earnestly, if imperfectly, sought to serve Christ through my works. I have been "doing for Christ," all my life, and only recently God has made me see how little of His saving grace was attached to all my energetic "spiritual" activity. The deaths of my sister and father placed me in God's crucible, where His refining fire continues to peel away my self-righteousness, drawing me back to His Word and His very words – "Take heart! I have overcome the world."*

These poems are the result of my walk through fire, where I now find myself standing here, a learner at the Cross, holding tightly to Christ, like Jacob wrestling with God, waiting for His blessing. * (NIV)

Susan E. Erikson

Susan E. Erikson (Master of Arts, Historical Theology, Westminster Seminary California) has been married for thirty-eight years, raised three children, and is the proud grandmother of ten. She writes choral music, and many of her pieces have been performed by the New Life Presbyterian Church, Escondido adult choir, where she has been the director since 2000. She is also the author of a women's leadership training program that has been used in five churches, and presently serves as Chair, Christian Growth with New Life's women's ministries. She and her husband live in Escondido, California. This is her first published book of poetry.

Susan

Marilyn

Marilyn D. Segraves (B.A., Art Education, U.C.L.A.; California Life Secondary Teaching Credential; additional 64 units from U.C.S.D. and Westminster Seminary California) taught art at the high school and adult school levels for fourteen years. She has also worked as a designer, illustrator, and graphic artist. She was represented in galleries in six states and participated in exhibits throughout California until 1990 when she felt the Lord calling her into media production work. She has since created hundreds of productions for Christian and non-profit organizations, winning numerous awards. She and her husband live in Escondido, California.

www.ingramcontent.com/pod-product-compliance
Lightning Source LLC
Chambersburg PA
CBHW041801160426
43191CB00001B/4